YOUR KNOWLEDGE HAS VALUE

Bibliographic information published by the German National Library:

The German National Library lists this publication in the National Bibliography; detailed bibliographic data are available on the Internet at http://dnb.dnb.de .

Imprint:

Copyright © 2012 GRIN Verlag
Print and binding: Books on Demand GmbH, Norderstedt Germany
ISBN: 9783346268198

This book at GRIN:

https://www.grin.com/document/304542

Luca Kaiser

China's Integration into the Greek Economy. A Case Study of the Port of Piraeus

GRIN Verlag

GRIN - Your knowledge has value

Since its foundation in 1998, GRIN has specialized in publishing academic texts by students, college teachers and other academics as e-book and printed book. The website www.grin.com is an ideal platform for presenting term papers, final papers, scientific essays, dissertations and specialist books.

Visit us on the internet:

http://www.grin.com/

http://www.facebook.com/grincom

http://www.twitter.com/grin_com

China's Integration into the Greek Economy:
A Case Study of the Port of Piraeus

Term Paper by

Luca Raphaël Arvid Kaiser

December 21, 2012

Introduction

The port of Piraeus is the largest and most important port in Greece and one of largest ports in the Mediterranean. The port acts as a main gate for Greek imports and exports and plays a vital role in the national economy (Piraeus Port Authority SA [OLP], 2012). After the initial growth of the port, the transshipment volume decreased significantly from 2006 due to competing transshipment hubs in the eastern Mediterranean (Psaraftis & Pallis, 2012). In addition, the economic crisis has had a severe impact on seaports. Container traffic in Piraeus decreased by over 50% in 2008 (OLP, 2012).

Due to past economic policies, Greece has entered a severe economic crisis. High debt levels in combination with high budget deficits have contributed to Greece's current economic crisis. However, we have to consider that countries such as the USA and Japan are also deeply in debt and have large deficits, but do not face a crisis similar to that in Greece. Contrary to the widespread reports in the mass media, the underlying factor is not the wastefulness of Greece's public authorities, but the lack of competitiveness, intensified by the Euro and global crises and the resulting lack of confidence in Greece's capitalism (Sakellaropoulos, 2010, pp. 322-324).

While Greece has experienced negative annual GDP growth rates since 2009, China's average GDP has grown annually since 2009 at a rate of almost 10% (World Bank, 2012a). China's economic rise has led to a take-off in Foreign Direct Investments (FDI) in Europe by Chinese companies. According to Hanemann and Rosen (2012), the number of deals exceeding one million USD doubled from less than 50 in 2007 to almost 100 in 2011. They further show that Greece, together with Hungary, was the country with the highest increase in the share of total inward FDI from China in the European Union (EU) compared to the rest of the world from 2000 to 2011. The main reason for this increase was one large-scale deal.

In 2009, the state-controlled China Ocean Shipping Company (COSCO) committed to a long-term lease of half of the port of Piraeus (fully taking over the operation of Pier II in June 2010), which was tied to an immediate investment of over 700 million USD (Hanemann & Rosen, 2012, p. 38; Psaraftis & Pallis, 2012, p. 17). The other half of the port (Pier I) is still run by Greece, resulting in novel intra-port competition.

The privatization of half of the port and the Chinese involvement was controversial from the outset. Psaraftis and Pallis (2012, p. 17) explain that the contract was ratified several times and lawsuits were filed including with the Supreme Court. Concerns regarding legal provisions included various tax exemptions and other standard obligations which would be more favorable to COSCO than to the Piraeus Port Authority SA (OLP) or other Greek institution, raising questions in terms of the fairness of the upcoming competition between the two entities. In October 2009, several strikes by the port unions shut down the container terminal for two months (eased due to the fact that elections were coming up). Psaraftis and Pallis (2012, p. 17) state that the main concerns of Greece's powerful labor unions relate to the salaries and working rules of existing personnel and the hiring of new personnel under different conditions.

The case study of the port of Piraeus can be linked to numerous current development debates and provides an ideal base for examination of a much broader phenomenon: the new global order with an emerging China and a struggling Europe. Is China taking advantage of the economic crisis in Greece? If so, does it matter? There are two different views concerning China's integration in the port of Piraeus: Whilst the port unions accuse the Chinese of bringing third world labor standards to Europe, others state that China's investments create an economic opportunity for a country in crisis. Hence, this paper will explore China's integration in the port of Piraeus and aims to answer the question of whether it is a curse or blessing for the development of the port of Piraeus and in a broader sense for Greece. The paper will attempt to achieve this by analyzing the two different views and linking them with current debates and prevailing theories in development.

Global Integration or Penetration?

Besides the successful transition from a planned socialist economy to a market economy and several pragmatic and effective market-oriented reforms, China's growth has been based on resource-driven growth, namely, cheap labor and the connected rapid labor-force growth, with declining birth rates bringing down dependency rates (Naughton, 2007).

However, due to its rapidly aging population, China is facing a labor shortage in the future. The resulting change of labor supply and demand will lead to higher wages in China. To combat the upward pressure on wages brought on by a labor shortage, Chinese manufacturers need to move up the global value chain (Hamlin, 2011). To do so, Chinese companies need to go beyond China's borders. To move from low value manufacturing to the higher profit margins afforded by distribution and serve overseas customers directly, China needs to invest more in overseas markets (Hanemann & Rosen, 2012, p. 29). China's deal with the Greek government to run part of the port of Piraeus is part of a larger strategy with broader objectives and is in compliance with COSCO's goal to transform from a shipping carrier into 'a global logistic player' (Wei Jiafu, president of the COSCO Group, cited in Wang, 2005). Although the port of Piraeus is small compared to the top ten European ports by volume, it is closer for ships transporting goods from China to Europe through the Suez Canal than northern sea ports in Europe. Moreover, the port is closer to emerging markets such as Turkey, Russia, and the Balkan states. COSCO is promising to more than double container traffic in Piraeus to 3.7 million twenty-foot equivalent units (TEUs) by 2015 and both governments emphasize the mutual benefits (Mihalakas, 2011).

Despite the positive outlook, labor unions were against the deal ab initio. This creates the impression that FDI from China or any Chinese involvement in global politics brings criticism. It is widely held that countries should create perfect conditions for international investment and build a business-friendly environment in order to develop. Yet, it seems that some western media outlets, politicians, and the population at large are upset if the investor turns out to be Chinese. This raises the question of whether a new form of orientalism is emerging. Vukovich (2012) argues that Sino-orientalism shifted from 'being different' to 'being the same', pointing out the cultural logic of capitalism in the new interpretation of China. It is our own kind that we fear – being nothing but afraid of what the West created: global capitalism. Global competitiveness, promoted by capitalist economies to maintain and reproduce capitalist hegemony within the advanced capitalist countries themselves (Cammack, 2006), does not seem appropriate when applied by so-called less advanced or emerging economies. During the 2012 US presidential debate, China was mentioned a dozen times – all in a negative context. This negative attitude is also reflected with regard to Chinese "aid" in Africa, which is mainly associated with the exploitation of natural resources, but not to investments in infrastructure, the setting up of business ties, and so on (c.f. Brautigam, 2009).

China's form of "aid", which is mainly a form of FDI, is no less questionable than "western aid". Taking Glennie's (2008, p. 104) approach towards aid, it is solely a cost-efficient way of buying economic advantage and political support. Pannell (2008, p. 708) states that the driving force behind China's interest in outflowing FDI is to attain foreign markets for Chinese goods in order to create jobs for Chinese citizens both at home and abroad to maintain social and political stability in China. Although Pannel (2008) is referring to Africa in his article, one could assume that his case is even more applicable to Europe because of the higher purchasing power. Nevertheless, besides a handful of Chinese managers, China did not import any workers in COSCO's case to Piraeus (Alderman, 2012), negating the assumption that locals have to compete with Chinese workers. However, it seems that the Chinese government considers weak economies easier to deal with than stronger ones. Greece's current economic crisis has provided an excellent opportunity to enter the Greek economy and to create economic advantage to bring Chinese goods to Europe.

Labor Standards

There are two port unions in Greek: the Federation of Permanent Employees of Greek Ports (OMYLE) and the Federation of Cargo Handlers of Greece (OFE) (Psaraftis & Pallis, 2012, p. 9). All port personnel actively participate in the labor unions. The labor unions have found a common enemy in the terminal's privatization, mainly because they believe that labor rights are less secure under a private company.

Alderman (2012) reports that the director of OLP, the port unions, and former workers accuse COSCO of lowering safety measures to save money, using employment subcontractors who hire temporary, unskilled, nonunion workers who are desperately seeking jobs, exploiting them by paying minimum wages, and giving minimal training despite the dangerous nature of the job. Furthermore, she gives the example of a COSCO dockworker who was fired because he raised concerns about safety violations and tried to organize a workers' committee. They also blame COSCO for 'bringing third world labor standards to Europe'.

However, whilst the Chinese side of the port is booming, the Greek run side of the port is struggling and its business lags far behind (Alderman, 2012). To some extent, this can be traced back to the different labor rules on the two sides. Labor rules on the Greek side are less flexible and the workers enjoy much higher wages and protection (Alderman, 2012). Referring to Alderman (2012), the salaries of some workers reached $ 181,000 per year, whereas COSCO typically pays less than $ 23,200 per year. Psaraftis and Pallis (2012, p. 9) confirm the incredibly high salaries on Greek side and relate them to obsolete labor regulations. Alderman (2012) further argues that while COSCO uses four workers to work a gantry crane, the labor union requires nine employees to be used on the Greek side.

Pallis (2007, p. 233) maintains that politicians have tended to exercise social policies at Greek ports. In 1997, the OLP was obliged to spend almost 20% of its annual income to retired port workers. In the 1980s the minimum wage in Greece was among the highest within OECD countries in Europe (Bournakis, 2009, p. 124). Bournakis (2009, pp. 124-148) cites the bargaining power of trade unions and the active role of the welfare state as the main reasons for the high minimum wages. He explains that the agreed minimum wage under the influence of powerful trade unions resulted in higher labor costs compared to competing countries, which led to a decline in productivity growth. He further states that, besides adjustments in the 1990s, trade unions have maintained their strong bargaining power, which has prevented structural reform implementation in favor of a more flexible labor market. He claims that the welfare state has negative effects on productivity growth and entrepreneurship because it prevents firms from aligning their work force quickly and effectively. Matsaganis (2011) confirms this and sees the welfare state in Greece as among the causes of the economic crisis.

"We came here and wanted to help the locals [with] fast developing. But the Europeans, they think they should be enjoying their life. So most of the people want to go on more holidays but from the other side they want to reduce the working time" (Fu, COSCO Chief Executive, Piraeus, 2012).

The Bank of Greece (2012) states that Greece's cost competitiveness has increased since 2010 and considers the lower labor costs as a main factor. According to the bank's annual report, average unit labor costs used to increase annually and were notably higher than the average increase in unit labor costs in the Euro area. In 2008, annual average unit labor costs increased by a tremendous 8.7% (compared to 3.7% in the Euro area). In 2010 and 2011, however, for the very first time, unit labor costs decreased by 3.8% and 2.6% respectively. The Bank of Greece further predicted that the unit labor costs would decrease by up to 6.8% in 2012, which seems in line with the bank's goal to increase competitiveness. Furthermore, the Bank of Greece (2012) has advised the government to create a business-friendly environment and speed up the privatization program to attract FDI and to increase competitiveness.

In sum, the aforementioned arguments express a very neo-classical view of development. Therefore, the function of the Greek government should be limited to the provision of a business-friendly environment and, based on Adam's Smith invisible hand, let private firms determine supply and demand in markets, which is in the best interests of society. However, on the basis of Karl Marx's idea, I argue that the invisible hand is indeed routed through capital lending institutions, for instance, banks. Its interests is solely based on the principles of capitalism underlying investment decisions – seeking profit, moving capital from low to highly profitable companies, and putting pressure on a company's input costs, namely, labor. In Karl Marx's view, in a society based on private interests, even the wealthiest state of society leads to the suffering of the working class and is therefore not in the best interests of society. The prevalent neo-liberal view held by the Bank of Greece promotes the proletarianization of the poor by arguing for an environment in which the poor are mobilized and exploited to work, justified by the prospect of future economic growth (Cammack, 2008, pp. 136-137).

The case of Piraeus has shown that COSCO's operation has created new jobs and provides around 1,000 jobs for Greek workers (Alderman, 2012). Even more remarkable, most workers are willing to accept new conditions such as lower wages and less job security. In the words of Hatzakos (2012), the general director of the OLP, 'Employees think twice about strikes and labor action now'.

The current economic crisis and social transformation of the global division of labor have led to aggressive class policies such as wage cuts, greater labor flexibility, a loosening of restrictions on firing, and a reduction in pensions. Subject to capitalist formations of higher productivity, the Greek working class will have to learn to cope (Sakellaropoulos, 2010).

It seems that in a capitalist system, the prevailing question is whether it is better to have no job or to have a low paid job with low job security.

Competition and Efficiency

It is most likely that the current economic crisis in Greece has created an opportunity for China to enter the Greek economy and to implement low labor costs. Yet, from a more long-term perspective, we have to ask: Even if China is taking advantage of the economic crisis in Greece, does it matter? COSCO is spending millions of dollars modernizing its docks to increase its container loads and to become one of the world's largest ports (Alderman, 2012). Moreover, COSCO will construct a third pier (Pier III) by 2015 (Psaraftis & Pallis, 2012).

Before the Chinese entered the market, OLP, the Greek operator of Pier I, did not face any local competition. Between 1996 and 2000, OLP could double its container traffic. However, despite the beneficial location of Piraeus and a further boom in maritime freight trade between 2000 and 2008, growth stagnated (Psaraftis & Pallis, 2012, p. 9). Ambition and reality were a long way from each other. The absence of local competition resulted in significant malfunctioning of the port and Piraeus started to lose a large share of its container traffic to competing regional transport hubs such as those in Malta, Cyprus, Spain, Italy, and Egypt (Psaraftis & Pallis, 2012, p. 7). These ports introduced reforms to develop advanced logistic strategy and specialization (Psaraftis & Pallis, 2012, p. 9). According to the OLP, inefficient operational costs considerably exceeded the standard costs of its competitors.

Run down as a state-run enterprise, under Chinese leadership the port's productivity has flourished and the cargo volume has tripled since 2010 (Alderman, 2012). It can be assumed that the new competition for the Greek port authority will require them to find better ways of operating. Earlier, I gave the example of the number of people required to work a gantry crane on the Greek side (9 workers) and the Chinese side (4 workers). The outcome is simple: OLP will need to harmonize and adjust current business strategies or it will be unable to compete with COSCO. Psaraftis and Pallis (2012, p. 20) state that 'OLP will have to push for reforms that are long overdue'. The emerging competition results in a convergence of input prices towards marginal costs, leading to efficiency gains and a more rational division of labor on the Greek side. This may result in temporary job losses. According to the World Bank (2012b, p. 10), economic growth happens when jobs become more productive, but also as less productive jobs disappear. In order to create more jobs in the long run, OLP will need to create an extra profit margin and invest in new technologies and innovation. According to Mankiw and Taylor (2008, p. 371), technological advance raises the product margins of labor, which eventually increases the demand for labor. Hence, employment might expand, despite rising wages.

I herewith close this section with an example given by the famous Austrian economist Joseph A. Schumpeter in 1939:

> "[...] for instance, a small tailor decides to employ a specialist in sewing on buttons because, and only because, his business expands" (Schumpeter, 1939, p. 89).

Competition and Innovation

Intense criticism of ports not only focused on the inefficiency of ports in Greece, but also on the absence of innovative ideas by port managers (Pallis, 2007). Technological development in ports may include new logistical organization or 'door-to-door' chains, by linking the mode of sea transport with land transport, as well as efficient electronic information exchange between ship, port, and land transport (Reynaud, 2004). A port must seek its own way of specialization and develop a different production model in order to be superior to other ports (Langen & Pallis, 2006).

Thus, after defining the impact of intra-port competition on economic efficiency, I will further analyze the impact of competition on innovation. According to Schumpeter's theory of economic development (2006), innovation is a key factor in economic development and the only effective form of competition. The Schumpeterian growth theory implies a negative impact of perfect competition on innovation. Schumpeter argued that some level of monopoly power is required for innovation because monopolies are more likely to invest in innovation due to higher profit margins. Only by innovating continuously can a monopoly maintain its position. Hence, innovation is an ever existing "threat", meaning competing by inventing, whereas under perfect competitive conditions all players in an industry would eventually produce the same goods for the same price with the same technologies. Applying this theory, the essential question is therefore whether one of the port sides can maintain a monopoly – this is more likely to be COSCO due to higher current investments in infrastructure and current performance – and contribute to the port's development by accelerating the innovation process. Yet, if the Greek side were able to economize on the division of labor and enhance efficiency, intra-port competition might lower total profits and profit margins on both sides, implying that there is little scope for innovation and spending for Research and Development (R&D). Hence, intra-port competition in Piraeus may create a disadvantage against competing ports because it restrains the innovative process.

Bertschek (1995) on the other hand, points out the positive effects of FDI on the innovative activity of domestic firms. Due to increased competition in domestic markets, domestic companies have to find ways to maintain their market position. Hence, competition not only leads to economic efficiency gains, but also puts pressure on innovation, in turn also leading to productivity growth in the long run.

Yawawaki (1993) notes the reverse relationship of the above-mentioned case. He claims that in terms of Japanese FDI during the late 1980s in Europe, the driving forces behind FDI outflow were the large R&D capacity, low labor costs, and the large market size in the recipient country. This has some similarities with our case study, taking into account advanced technological capabilities in Europe and the innovative spill-over effect, the opportunity to introduce lower labor costs in the case of Greece, and the attraction of the European market for Chinese goods.

In line with Schmutzler (2010), who states that increasing competition can have a positive or negative impact on R&D investments and hence the innovation process, I argue that it is barely possible to predict the development of the innovation level of the two port competitors in Piraeus.

However, I believe that the lack of local competition has led to mediocrity and the avoidance of costly innovation in the case of Piraeus. Moreover, monopolies and imperfect competition hamper innovation because they create fewer incentives and higher barriers for new competitors or innovators to enter the market. Despite counter arguments and different theoretical conceptions, I consider that perfect competition and low entrance barriers for (foreign) competitors and FDI increase innovative activities, but also, vice versa, that innovative activities in domestic markets attract FDI. In the case of competition at the port of Piraeus, I see competition as driving force behind future modernization and innovation. COSCO is investing in electromechanical equipment and is delivering full mechanical equipment to increase container capacity (Psaraftis & Pallis, 2012, p. 14), which will force the Greek side to seek its own path of modernization in order to catch up with COSCO.

Conclusion

China's global economic integration is often perceived as negative. Instead of fearing China's rising economic power, it is time to acknowledge the positive role of China in the world economy. There is vast welfare potential from Chinese investment – fresh capital, taxes, innovation spill-overs, and jobs. Chinese firms currently employ more than 45,000 Europeans (Hanemann & Rosen, 2012).

Greece, isolated from the rest of Western Europe and disadvantaged in terms of profiting from the EU due to inferior competitive advantage compared to northern European countries, needs FDI to strengthen the economy, become more competitive, and to benefit as transporting hub. China's exports to the EU in 2011 amounted to 292.1 billion Euros (European Commission [EC], 2012). Even if China decides only to use the port of Piraeus for a quarter of its total exports to Europe, it will provide great economic opportunities for Greece. The competition between the two sides will economize labor division, enhance efficiency, and increase technological progress, in turn affecting productivity on both sides. As a result, the port of Piraeus will be able to compete with or even outpace other ports in the Mediterranean, advancing towards the status of Europe's top ports. Chinese investment will contribute to making Greece the main south-European entrance port for Chinese goods and hence boost the Greek economy, finally mutually benefiting both countries.

However, such a positive outcome is far from certain and will almost certainly not be smooth. Although I believe in a positive outcome from the privatization of the Port of Piraeus and the entrance of the Chinese company, there are various long-term social and economic events and systems which will influence the outcome. Exogenous impacts include, but are not limited to, the development of the current economic crisis in Greece, austerity measures imposed by the EU, China's future economic growth and any changes in regulation in (maritime freight) trade. In addition, the decrease in labor standards may result in a new wave of protests. COSCO must secure a safe working environment and maintain Europe's rule of law. However, the port's labor union must acknowledge a certain change in labor standards and let go of obsolete concessions in order to overcome the recession and to create new jobs in the long run.

The top-down approach of the Chinese company is what Greece should aspire to in times of a crisis like this. If Greece seeks to avoid dependence on its northern European neighbors, it must become more competitive. In order to achieve this, it must remove labor market regulations, privatize state assets, and attract foreign investment (but avoid imperfect competition), which will in turn create new jobs. According to the World Bank (2012b), jobs do not only increase economy-wide productivity growth, but also reduce poverty and enhance individuals' well-being. Acknowledging the flaws and problems arising from the liberal problem-solving approach, the absence of a profound alternative, especially in the case of Greece, already deeply integrated in the global economy, leads to my conclusion.

Unfortunately, the costs of the current crisis are transferred to the forces of living labor. However, I consider economic growth and social well-being as virtuous circle. Based on Amartya Sen's Capability Approach, since an individual's welfare depends on the amount of money at his disposal and a nation's welfare depends on the amount of money at its disposal, hence GDP, I see productivity growth as the ultimate goal for Greece. Once Greece achieves gradual GDP growth and is released from recession, it needs to focus on additional issues in relation to GDP growth such as new forms of social protection (consistent with competitiveness), to fulfill the needs of its citizens.

Bibliography

Alderman, L. (2012). *Under Chinese, a Greek Port Thrives.* October 10. Retrieved December 6, 2012, from The New York Times Online-Website: http://www.nytimes.com/2012/10/11/business/global/chinese-company-sets-new-rhythm-in-port-of-piraeus.html?pagewanted=all&_r=0

Bank of Greece. (2012). *SUMMARY OF THE ANNUAL REPORT 2011.* Athens: Bank of Greece.

Bertschek, I. (1995). PRODUCT AND PROCESS INNOVATION AS A RESPONSE TO INCREASING IMPORTS AND FOREIGN DIRECT-INVESTMENT. *Journal of industrial economics,* 43(4), pp. 341-357.

Bournakis, I. (2009). *Competitiveness Trade and Productivity: With Special Reference to Greece.* Saarbrücken: VDM Verlag Dr. Müller.

Brautigam, D. (2009). *The Dragon's Gift, The Real Story of China in Africa.* Oxford: Oxford University Press.

Cammack, P. (2006). *The politics of global competitiveness.* Papers in the Politics of Global Competitiveness, No. 1, Institute for Global Studies, Manchester Metropolitan University, e-space Open Access Repository.

Cammack, P. (2008). Poverty policy and the politics of competitiveness. In P. Kennett, *Governance, Globalization and Public Policy* (pp. 131-150). Cheltenham: Edward Elgar Publishing Limited.

European Commission [EC]. (2012). *Bilateral relations China.* December 3. Retrieved December 7, 2012, from European Commission-Website: http://ec.europa.eu/trade/creating-opportunities/bilateral-relations/countries/china/

Fu, C. Q. (2012). COSCO Chief Executive, Piraeus Container Terminal. October 2. Interview for the New York Times. (L. Alderman, Interviewer)

Glennie, J. (2008). *The Trouble with Aid: Why less Could Mean More for Africa.* London: Zed Books.

Hamlin, K. (2011). *China's One-Child Policy Is Crippling Industry.* September 8. Retrieved December 7, 2012, from Bloomberg Businessweek-Website: http://www.businessweek.com/magazine/chinas-onechild-policy-is-crippling-industry-09082011.html

Hanemann, T., & Rosen, D. H. (2012). *China Invests in Europe: Patterns, Impacts and Policy Implications.* New York, NY: Rhodium Group, LLC.

Hatzakos, S. (2012). *Under Chinese, a Greek Port Thrives.* October 2. (L. Alderman, Interviewer) Piraeus: The New York Times.

Langen, P. W., & Pallis, A. A. (2006). Analysis of the Benefits of Intra-Port Competition. *International Journal of Transport Economics,* 33(1), pp. 69-85.

Mankiw, N. G., & Taylor, M. P. (2008). *Economics.* London: Cengage Learning EMEA.

Matsaganis, M. (2011). The welfare state and the crisis: the case of Greece. *Journal of European Social Policy,* 21(5), pp. 501-512.

Mihalakas, N. (2011). *China's investments in Greece are creating economic opportunities for both nations.* February 15. Retrieved December 7, 2012, from nl-aid-website: http://www.nl-aid.org/domain/economic/china%E2%80%99s-investments-in-greece-are-creating-economic-opportunities-for-both-nations/

Naughton, B. (2007). *The Chinese Economy: Transition and Growth.* Cambridge, MA: The MIT Press.

Pallis, A. A. (2007). Port governance models: Financial evaluation of Greek port restructuring. *TRANSPORT POLICY,* 14(3), pp. 232-246.

Pannell, C. W. (2008). China's Economic and Political Penetration in Africa. *EURASIAN GEOGRAPHY AND ECONOMICS,* 49(6), pp. 706-730.

Piraeus Port Authority SA [OLP]. (2012). *Strategy - Vision.* Retrieved December 5, 2012, from Piraeus Port Authority-Website: http://www.olp.gr/en

Psaraftis, H., & Pallis, A. (2012). Concession of the Piraeus container terminal: turbulent times and the quest for competitiveness. *Maritime Policy & Management,* 39(1), pp. 27-43.

Reynaud, C. (2004). *Ports of the Mediterranean.* Published in IEMed Yearbook 2003. Barcelona: European Institute for the Mediterranean (IEMed).

Sakellaropoulos, S. (2010). The Recent Economic Crisis in Greece and the Strategy of Capital. *Journal of Modern Greek Studies,* 28(2), pp. 321-348.

Schmutzler, A. (2010). *The relation between competition and innovation – Why is it such a mess?* Working Paper 0716. Zurich: Socioeconomic Institute, University of Zurich.

Schumpeter, A. J. (1939). *BUSINESS CYCLES: A Theoretical, Historical and Statistical Analysis of the Capitalist Process.* New York, NY et al.: McGraw-Hill Book Company.

Schumpeter, J. (2006). In J. Röpke, & O. Stiller, *Theorie zur wirtschaftlichen Entwicklung: Nachdruck der 1. Auflage von 1912 (Reprinting of 1st Edition in 1912).* Berlin: Duncker & Humblot.

Vukovich, D. F. (2012). *China and Orientalism: Western Knowledge Production and the P.R.C.* London et al.: Routledge.

Wang, Y. (2005). *TNT agrees to venture with COSCO.* Retrieved December 7, 2012, from China Daily Online-Website: http://www.chinadaily.com.cn/english/doc/2005-11/15/content_494761.htm

World Bank. (2012a). *World Development Indicators (WDI) & Global Development Finance (GDF).* Retrieved December 6, 2012, from World dataBank.

World Bank. (2012b). *World Development Report 2013: Jobs.* Washington, DC: International Bank for Reconstruction and Development / The World Bank.

Yawawaki, H. (1993). Location Decisions of Japanese Multinational Firms in European Manufacturing Industries. In K. Hughes, *European Competitiveness* (pp. 11-28). Cambridge: Cambridge University Press.